Copyright © 2011 by Colin Drake

First Edition

All rights reserved. No part of this book shall be reproduced or transmitted, for commercial purposes, without written permission from the author.

ISBN: 978-0-9871655-3-4

Also by the same author:

Beyond the Separate Self

The End of Anxiety and Mental Suffering

A Light Unto Your Self

Self Discovery Through
Investigation of Experience

Humanity Our Place in the Universe
The Central Beliefs of
The Worlds Religions

These titles are available as: e-books from www.nonduality.com and as Paperbacks from www.lulu.com

Contents

Introduction – Why Poetry?..3
Prologue --- The Power of Poetry..7
1   When We Say I……………………………..…..............15
2   Our Life is a Continual Flow………………........18
3   Awareness is Forever Here……………………..21
4   Who Am I?..24
5   Awareness is Nothing Special ……………………...27
6   At Home………………………...……………………..30
7   Nothing Matters ……………………………………..33
8   Relax………………………………………………….....36
9   Mantra…………………………………………..……...40
10 Everything Reveals Absolute Reality …………....43
11 Nothing to Do, No Problem to Solve……………….46
12 So What? …………………………………………….49
13 The Cart Before The Horse……………………….....52
14 Freedom……………………………………………….55
15 The Full Potential……………………………………58
16 The Best of All Worlds, Humanity at its Peak……..61
17 'This' ………………………………………………….64
18 'That'…………………………………………………..66

Introduction

Why Poetry?

I have been asked why write poetry after three books of prose? This was caused by a particularly intransigent questioner who was just not really hearing anything I was saying. He is an earnest spiritual seeker who has been searching for over forty years but who is dominated by identification with his mind, which has left him totally confused. He was continually asking for 'proof' of what I was pointing to, without really being prepared to investigate, with an open mind, for himself. So finally in desperation I wrote the following:

You Ask For Proof

You ask for proof,

What more proof could there be?

That which lives and breathes in me,

Also lives and breathes in thee.

The Lover and Beloved are ever within and without,

Of this amazing Mystery there can be no doubt.

She feels every sensation that our bodies feel,

As we eat She partakes of every meal.

That which we hear and see,

Is also heard and seen by the Beloved, Thee.

All that we taste and smell,

Is sensed, through us, by Thee as well.

Every thought with which our minds resound,

In Thy infinite Cosmic Mind is found.

For behind every conscious body/mind,

The Seer, Knower and Enjoyer can we find.

Moreover, not a thought nor sensation escapes,

Without appearing in Thy universal 'tapes'.

Within each of us our experiences are 'recorded',

By which device awareness of them is afforded.

In this there can be no separate 'saying',

Manifestation is the Lover and Beloved playing.

What appears to us as 'you' and 'me',

Are wondrous instruments of the Beloved, Thee.

In the manifest and unmanifest there is no separation,

The realization of which needs no preparation.

For the Lover and Beloved are already one,

Appearing as the 'many' just for fun!

Alas, this also did not get through, although he did say it was a nice poem, which was much more affirmative than the usual cynicism and scepticism he brought to our conversations.

However, when I e-mailed this poem out it evoked the most number of positive responses I have ever received from a mail out. When discussing this with a poet friend of mine he asserted that poetry has the potential to be more powerful than prose, as it is more condensed and thus requires the reader to investigate its meaning more than prose, which tends to put the meaning 'on a plate'. As my writings are always an exhortation for the readers to investigate the Truth for themselves I was greatly attracted to this and I think that it has some validity.

As you will see from the prologue this was born out when one of my poems 'hit home', which greatly encouraged me to write more. So I decided to write poems based on chapters of my first book *Beyond the Separate Self* (which has been very well received) for those that prefer the poetic approach.

Each poem should be read slowly and carefully not moving onto the next quatrain (four line verse) until you have fully 'got' what is being offered. This may require some investigation and contemplation which is all the better for then the meaning will be your own discovery that the quatrain has pointed you to. Do not move onto the next poem until you have spent some time contemplating and considering the present one.

If you have any questions you can contact me on colin108@dodo.com.au , or alternatively buy the prose version of *Beyond the Separate Self* online at www.nonduality.com or in paperback at www.lulu.com

Prologue

The Power of Poetry

The following shows how poetry may point one to awakening:

Here is an e-mail I sent to Hanumandass who was struggling with 'how to apply nondual awareness to the phenomenal world' :

From: Colin Drake
Sent: Tuesday, June 07, 2011 3:56 PM
To: Hanumandass

Hi, In response to your comment that : *I've been struggling lately with how to apply nondual awareness to the phenomenal world.*

As far as I have experienced one does not 'apply' this in the normal sense of the word, for once one is established in this nondual awareness then this transforms one's interactions with the physical world, requiring no conscious application:

Awakening is Immensely Practical

Awakening is immensely practical,
Transformative rather than tactical.
Existential angst does it banish,
This fear and anxiety totally vanish.

In this life unfolds with no personal 'story'.
Then manifestation appears in all its glory.
When the world is met with a clear mind,
So vivid and alive do it we find.

Every sensation comes on so strong,
When not filtered through what's 'right and wrong'.
Thus seeing things as they truly 'are'
Our opinionated ego cannot mar.

When each moment is directly met,
The past and future go we let.
When the mind is still it does not distort,
So our experience does not fall short.

Sat-Chit-Ananda is another name,

For the source and essence of this cosmic game.

Sat – 'What is', Chit – Awareness of this,

Ananda – of this awareness the Bliss.

When awake we respond, rather than react,

To each situation depending on the fact.

Spontaneously does the mind our problems solve,

If unclouded by self it will not 'revolve'.

So I urge you all to awake,

Abandon self-image the great fake.

Investigate, discover what's really here,

Leading to a life with no angst and fear!

Cheers, Colin Drake

'

Below follows his response, with my comments in italics (which were sent to him) plus my response:

From: Hanumandass

Sent: Wednesday, June 08, 2011 6:27 AM
To: Colin Drake
Subject: Re: Awakening is Immensely Practical

Colin,

Firstly, thank you from the bottom of my heart for contacting me. I was at work last night when I received your email. I was familiar with your name but not with your work. However I read your poem (I assume that's what it was) quite casually to begin with. By the time I was into the second or third line something profound happened, or rather didn't happen.

I can only express it in terms of experience for I know no better avenue. Upon reading 'Awakening is Immensely Practical' I experienced two things simultaneously. The first being that everything in my mind, the whirling caldron of thoughts trying vainly to unravel nondual awareness, fell away. The second experience that sort of accompanied this falling away was that of a deep sense of freedom.

Great!

Colin, I wish to neither underestimate the magnitude of what has happened over the last hours nor turn the events into some sort of divine impartation of grace from the beyond. What has happened to me is so horribly simple that I feel something of regret for the years of seemingly hopeless searching but at the same instant it's been the most spiritual REAL thing that has befallen me.

No need for regret, the years of searching have brought you to the point where you were totally ready just needing a gentle push to fall off the cliff, letting go of all your supports. Exactly the same thing happened to me ... see 'Spiritual Experience' in 'Beyond The Separate Self.' Also once you are awake the past is totally irrelevant!

Was it awakening? My mind is telling me no, that I ought to sort it all out and label it and find out if it's valid. Something is different now however. The mind continues its machinations, but it's like I am watching it all take place. And this is different because there is no effort to be a witness like it's a spiritual exercise. Surely I fall back into identification with the mind and the body but it only requires a remembrance of the awareness of it all to put me back into a serene witnessing of it ALL.

That's exactly what awakening is: becoming established in awareness of, and identification with, awareness itself. When the establishment is complete no remembrance will be required.

Also you have hit the nail on the head in that awareness witnesses without any (one) 'doing' taking place. Thoughts and sensations just arise, exist, are 'seen', and subside back into awareness itself.

My mind says no, my body says no, but the core of my being says YES. It feels like home. It's as if nothing has 'happened' I have merely began to rest in a recognition of awareness without any effort on 'my' part. When I reflect upon it it seems like an experience. But what's different from my other experiences is this state of being, awareness of 'what is' as you have put it, is right here. It only seems like an experience when I think about it or try to remember it, etc.

*That's absolutely right, 'awakening is not an experience' (see chapter of this name in 'A Light Unto Yourself') just a deep recognition of the fact that 'one **is** awareness'. This may engender many experiences, but freedom is obtained from cultivating, and honouring, this recognition.*

Also it is a true homecoming, to the place we can never leave, and actually have never left. For more of my thoughts on this see 'Home is Where the Heart is' in 'Beyond the Separate Self'.

My point in relating all this to you is twofold. Firstly I would like to ask you for your analysis since my mind keeps telling me no. And secondly, I don't know what caused you to contact me but I want you to know whatever the reason was you have done something no one else has been able to, point me to awakening.

The mind will keep saying 'no' until the establishment has taken place, as it is not in its interests to say yes, having for long held the place of honour (and power) as who you (think you) are. See 'Awareness of Awareness' in 'A Light Unto Yourself', the second half of which deals specifically with this problem.

Also, I don't know how busy you are but if you have the time I would love to exchange emails with you concerning nonduality, Advaita Vedanta, Buddhism, and mainly this transformation that has taken place in my life among other things.

Lastly I would like to have your permission to post the poem in question on my blog. It has obviously rocked my world and I feel it could do much for my readers.

Again thank you for contacting me, it meant more than you probably intended, but will have lasting effects on me and those around me. I'm going to download your books in a couple of days also, the least I could do for you!

It didn't mean more than I intended, in fact the result is exactly what I intended, but it certainly meant more than I had hoped for or expected.... which is great!

Sorry for the lengthy email. I hope it's reassurance that your effort to bare the simplest message of all has had an effect!

Sincerely,
Hanumandass

Dear Hanumandass, What a wonderful e-mail, It's such a joy (and relief) to hear that there is one less mind running around searching for the unfindable. Unfindable of course because it is always here and can never be lost, just overlooked to our cost. Your reply shows a clear appreciation of awakening, which if you read it back carefully will answer all of your own questions! Isn't that great ... However, I will add a few comments of my own, see below (above). Love, Colin

Poem One

When We Say I

This poem considers the problem with identifying oneself as a separate being.

When We Say 'I'

When we say 'I',

It's often a lie.

Denoting an apparently separate being,

From its looming extinction fleeing …

Fearing the engulfing nothingness,

In which there seems not more but less.

Avoided by expansion of image-self,

Acquiring more power, prestige and pelf*.

Alas this effort is all in vain,

For death annihilates this illusory gain.

This is the root of our anxiety and fear.

Transcend these see what's always Here!

Discover what at the core you really are,

This needs no prestigious fancy car!

Nor money, influence, name or fame,

Part and parcel of the great cosmic game.

That which sees our every thought,

Of which, at school, we are not taught,

In which all our sensations appear,

Without which we would not know they're here.

The constant conscious subjective presence,

Our innermost, fundamental, vital essence.

Which is ever aware of the turbulent flow

Of objects perceived as they come and they go.

Here complete stillness and silence reign,

Absolute peace with nothing to gain.

For this just witnesses the cosmic play,

Utterly untroubled by whatever may …

* Pelf - 'Money, especially when gained dishonestly' Oxford English Dictionary

Poem Two

Our Life is a Continuous Flow

This poem indicates a method of investigating one's moment to moment existence.

Our Life is a Continuous Flow

Our life is a continuous flow

Of experiences which just come and go.

Each of these has elements three,

Thoughts, sensations and that which these 'see'.

The first an ephemeral object-pair,

The latter the seer, ever aware.

The former arise, exist and subside

In awareness in which they ever reside.

So deeper than this material body/mind,

Is this sub-stratum so refined.

This conscious constant subjective core

Of which we can be ever sure.

Awareness is forever still,

Perceiving mind and sensations as they mill…

Utterly silent, without a sound,

In which that thought and heard are found.

Within this there is perfect peace.

For body/mind and objects cease

To indicate what, or who, we truly 'are'.

Thus our contentment they do not mar.

When we identify with this deeper level,

Emotions and feelings will not bedevil.

Witnessed scudding across the 'sky'

Of awareness which we can't deny.

Just watch them as they come and go,

Exhibiting a spectacular show.

Content, peaceful, ever at ease,

For what commences will always cease!

Poem Three

Awareness is Forever Here

This poem considers the properties that one can discover by investigating the nature of Awareness.

Awareness is Forever Here

Awareness is forever here,

In which mind and sensations appear.

Its presence is fundamental,

Absolute not incremental.

Choiceless, requiring no effort,

The seer of all that's thought.

All that our senses detect,

On this conscious 'screen' are decked.

Completely still without a sound,

Of every experience the 'ground'.

Perfectly peaceful under no duress,

Ever silent and utterly motionless.

Omnipresent, of consciousness the ocean.

Manifestation is This in motion.

All 'things' are forms of energy,

Arising from Its tranquility.

Omniscient, in which all things abide,

From which not one can ever hide.

The conscious stillness relative to which,

All movements are seen, without a hitch.

Omnipotent, back into which all things subside,

Stillness is the terminus of every 'ride'.

No thing can possibly affect It,

For they all appear, exist and exit.

Pure, for It manifestation cannot stain.

Pristine, for degradation It cannot feign.

Radiant, for by Its wondrous light,

The world appears to our mind's sight.

Poem Four

Who Am I ?

This poem points to what is discovered by self-inquiry.

Who Am I?

When we ask 'who am I?'

We discover by and by,

Absolutely nothing there,

Radiant, pristine, ever aware.

That by which our minds can know

Thoughts and sensations as they to and fro.

In which objects perceived are seen

Without which we wouldn't know they've been …

Once we actually realize who …

To awaken there's nothing to do,

For that which we truly are

Is right here, never afar.

Give up the search, still your mind

There's nothing left to find.

Awareness cannot be lost

Just overlooked to our great cost.

There's nothing to want or get.

That which we desire is met,

When we look deep within

Neath body, mind and all its din.

If awakening is what you truly seek

Under the ephemeral veil you must peek.

Once the discovery has taken place,

You can see your 'original face'.

Then you can totally let go,

Relax and enjoy the show.

Tranquil, content and ever at peace,

Let all 'becoming' finally cease!

Poem Five

Awareness is Nothing Special

This poem points to the fact that Awareness is absolutely normal, just overlooked, being the constant conscious subjective ground of being.

Awareness is Nothing Special

Awareness nothing special is,

Nondual there is only This.

Which effortlessly facilitates

Experience of ephemeral states.

Every object comes and goes,

Resting in its sweet repose.

So more extra-ordinary are they,

Than This, present come what may …

Underlying the universe,

And manifestation so diverse,

In which things arise and reside,

Back into which they all subside.

Abiding in its natural state,

Our consciousness so innate.

This which informs the mind

Of that which in the world we 'find'.

Alas the usual ego-state,

Tends Awareness to under-rate.

Searching for something more exotic,

Than this which we need not 'pick'.

Far and wide does the mind roam,

Deluded, missing its true home.

Seeking what's already here

Closer than close, nearer than near.

Just like a confused cattle drover,

Not realizing the search is over,

Whose herd he has already found,

Out seeking their tracks upon the ground!

Poem Six

At Home

This poem considers the fact that we are always At Home in the 'Essential Heart', and that we only imagine that we have left.

At Home

At home, in the essential Heart,

The central innermost vital part[1].

Here we flourish, live and reside,

Wherein there is no need to hide.

From which we can never leave,

Thus there is no need to grieve.

Imagining we have already left,

Evoking feelings so bereft.

This is part of the cosmic play.

Through which consciousness may,

Experience the amazing range,

Of thoughts and sensations as they change.

For if we continually stayed home,

Not allowed to seem to roam,

We would always be totally at peace,

So 'variety of life' would greatly decrease.

---

[1] One of the Oxford English Dictionary's definitions of 'Heart'.

This gives the secret clue,

When suffering, just ask 'who?'

Revealing that feelings come and go,

In That by which our minds can know.

In which mind and body appear,

By which, through us, That sees they're here,

From which we are never separate,

Awareness, our essence, so innate.

So to return home again,

To That which you need not attain.

See that you are This, never apart

From home, in the essential Heart!

Poem Seven

Nothing Matters

An investigation of the three meanings of 'Nothing Matters'.

Nothing Matters

Matters? No 'thing' ultimately does,

They arrive and depart on the cosmic bus.

In That in which they all arise,

Abide, and wherein each subsides.

That has taken on every form,

These come and go as the norm…

To know Itself in many a guise,

It dresses up in every disguise.

'Nothing' matters, is a vital key,

Relative to which all things we see.

Without which we could not know,

Thoughts and sensations as they flow.

Every thing is energy, thus is movement

In Consciousness needing no improvement.

Awareness is Its name when totally still,

Where there is 'nothing' for it to fill.

Before all movement there is rest.

Objects arise at That's behest.

In That they reside, Awareness itself,

To stillness they return, 'back onto the shelf'.

Thus nothing 'matters' for it creates,

As all motion arises from the still state.

Which contains all potential energy,

Manifesting as the universal synergy.

Therefore 'nothing matters' in each way,

For its three meanings that we can say.

So just relax, totally let ('things' come and) go,

Sit back and enjoy The Absolute's show!

Poem Eight

Relax

Elucidates the fact that relaxing, into Awareness, is the easiest way to awaken.

Relax

The easiest way to become wide awake,

Is to totally relax, for heaven's sake!

Into pure Awareness, your innermost essence,

Beneath body and mind with all its nonsense.

This simple mischievous thought,

Is liable to make the mind distraught.

Wondering how to achieve, or find, this state

And acquire the relaxation which I relate.

Don't worry, just apply this elegant test:

Am I aware of the thoughts with which I am blessed?

Or the sensations which in my body appear?

If 'yes' then Awareness is already here!

These fleeting objects appear on Its screen.

By viewing which they can be seen.

So body and mind exist at the surface level,

The deepest, Awareness, they cannot bedevil.

In this there can be no fear,

For Awareness is ever here.

This need not be achieved, found, or got,

Absent, lost, or missing It is not.

This is ever silent and still

Witnessing 'things' that seem to fill …

As This, we are always totally at peace,

Identification with body/mind completely cease.

So relax into That which we truly are,

Eternally carefree, never below par.

The cosmic audience of One,

Viewing its manifestation just for fun!

Strenuously seeking truth
by investigation and concentration,
one will never appreciate
the unthinkable simplicity and bliss
that abide at the core.

To uncover this fertile ground,
cut through the roots of complexity
with the sharp gaze of naked awareness,
remaining entirely at peace,
transparent and content.
You need not expend great effort
nor store up extensive spiritual power.
Remain in the flow of sheer awareness.

-Tilopa

Poem Nine

Mantra

How to use mantra repetition as a means to become aware of 'Aware Nothingness'.

Mantra

Though there is nothing to achieve, find, or get,

When 'awareness of Awareness' has been fully met;

For establishment of this ultimate knowing

Cultivation is required to aid its growing.

Butter comes from milk, as we all know,

But churning is required to make this so.

To keep one, of Awareness, enthused

Mantra repetition is a tool that can be used.

For this to be of use we must see

Of this technique the elements three:

The meaning of the mantra we repeat,

Awareness and Nothingness in this we meet.

"Om Namah Shivaya' is the one I employ,
For its profound meaning is a joy.
'Hail Pure Awareness', consciousness at rest,
Within which 'The Totality' is manifest.

As any mantra is practiced make sure to note
That you are aware of this, repeated by rote.
Recognition of Awareness is the vital key
Which this simple sadhana can help us see.

Also notice the nothingness, relative to which
The mantra is perceived in perfect pitch.
So as you repeat the phrase in your mind
Be aware of the nothingness in this you find.

Thus when this technique is skillfully performed,
Of 'Aware Nothingness' we become truly informed.
This is The Tao, Jehovah, Brahman, Allah, Rigpa – God
Revealed to mystics on the many paths they trod.

Poem Ten

Everything Reveals Absolute Reality

This poem considers the fact that every perception may reveal the nature of the Absolute Reality.

Everything Reveals Absolute Reality

If viewed in a certain way,

Every thing we perceive may

Directly reveal the Absolute Reality,

Underlying everyday 'normality'.

For behind every perception there must be

Two principles, easy to see.

Nothingness in which we know it's there,

And Awareness, so of it we are aware.

Consider a form sculpted from a single block,

Before the chiseling begins it's just a rock!

As the stone is removed revealing the space,

We are aware of the sculpture taking place.

Or a nightingale singing loud and clear.

If a band is playing we don't know it's here.

As soon as they have finished their set,

The song can be heard in the silence that's met.

Likewise for perception of any sensation,

This must be relative to its negation.

For any thought, or image, the mind to see,

On the screen of Awareness it must be.

The Absolute is That, consciousness at rest.

In which all things are manifest.

These are energy, ephemeral movements,

In That which brooks no improvements.

For perception of any thing to know,

In Awareness and Nothingness it must show.

These properties combined amount to That.

So every thing perceived reveals this fact!

Poem Eleven

Nothing to do, No Problem to Solve

Showing that with no problem to solve, and with the intent to recognise Awareness, the mind can become still.

Nothing to do, No Problem to Solve

Nothing to do, or problem to solve,

The recognition of Awareness to resolve.

For This is the constant conscious screen,

On which thoughts and sensations are seen.

The mind is a problem solving device,

Which quietens when there are none to entice.

When intent on identifying with the deeper level

Of Awareness, then thoughts will not bedevil.

This 'intent' is better than going to church,

To aid the mind in 'calling off the search'

For non existent problems to crack,

As in Awareness there is no lack.

Unless the mind is given a task,

It will probe, and spin and ask …

This 'intent' is a vital, precious clue

Which sets a task with 'nothing to do'.

When it is on a task intent,

The mind's meandering will relent.

In this it may well become still,

For there is nothing for it to fill.

When thus engaged it will not follow

Stray thoughts and feelings that 'show'.

These will just float across the sky

Of Awareness which it cannot deny.

With no problem to solve the mind can let go.

This sets the milieu in which it can know

The underlying constant conscious screen:

Awareness ever radiant, pure and pristine!

Poem Twelve

So What?

This poem considers how to live from Awareness of, or identification with, Awareness

So What?

If the peace of Awareness you have enjoyed,

Big deal, so what? Even now can you avoid

Life with all its ups and downs,

Tears and laughter, smiles and frowns?

The trick is to live from this deeper ground,

'Aware of Awareness', which you have found.

For this you need to fully commit,

To totally awaken, not just a bit …

You will tend to nod off again,

As ego its hold tries to regain.

Needing to wake up once more,

Awareness is the open door.

To aid in staying fully awake,

A bit of practice it does take.

Relaxing into Awareness thrice a day

Will help facilitate this, come what may.

It's best to remain totally alert,

So that any needless mental hurt,

Acts as a potent wake up call,

Thus back asleep one does not fall.

Let go the past, stay in the 'now'.

Awake with no 'story', that is how!

Also be completely 'here',

'Here and Now' life is so clear.

Accept it all, with no resistance,

Then life won't pall, nor will existence.

See the world as it 'is', wide awake,

Vivid and alive, make no mistake!

Poem Thirteen

The Cart Before the Horse

Elucidating the spiritual qualities that are the outcome of awakening.

The Cart Before the Horse

According to many paths on the spiritual 'roster',

To awaken there are qualities we need to foster.

But this is 'putting the cart before the horse',

When awake they appear as a matter of course.

Compassion is a matter of recognizing

We are the same, not just empathizing.

When awake it's easy to see

That I am you and you are me …

Discrimination between the 'real' and the 'unreal',

Means to see and know and 'feel'

The difference between Awareness, consciousness at rest,

And ephemeral objects, which in this manifest.

Love of God and ones' fellow 'men'

Results from seeing, when we awaken,

That 'all is one', for love is 'no separation'.

Awake this is clear, needing no preparation.

Contentment is remaining unperturbed

By things which, when 'asleep', we are disturbed.

Awareness is unaffected by what it's 'seeing'.

As This we exhibit that quality of being.

Detachment, that is not to cling

To anyone or any thing.

Awareness just witnesses 'what is'.

Awake, as That, one also does this.

Abandon sleep, Arise, Awake!

Dethrone the ego, just a fake…

Investigate, uncover what's always here,

Awareness, in which these qualities appear.

Poem Fourteen

Freedom

Showing that Freedom requires absolute commitment.

Freedom

Although Awareness you may have 'seen'
You may still say: 'My story must mean
Something profound about my essential being'.
Although discarding it is wonderfully freeing!

Now a decision you must make
Of which you would rather 'partake',
The level of ego, thoughts and the mind,
Or the Awareness in which these we find.

If the former level is that which you prefer,
Through a darkened filter the world you infer.
Whereas if the latter, abandoning the story,
Existence you perceive in all its glory.

For this to be absolutely so,
The past you must totally let go.
As, if about this you start to hedge,
Then this is 'the thin end of the wedge'.

When past feelings and memories flow

Just watch them as they come and they go,

With no story; then without a doubt

Their recurrences will slowly 'peter out'.

These can also act as an alarm bell

So that we do not fall back into hell.

Thus when they occur, if we stay awake

Needless suffering we can forsake.

Total vigilance is what is required,

To keep us, as Awareness, identified.

Finally 'All or Nothing' it must be,

To be absolutely and utterly free!

Weave not, like spiders, nets from grief's saliva
In which the woof and warp are both decaying.
But give the grief to Him, Who granted it,
And do not talk about it anymore.
When you are silent, His speech is your speech.
When you don't weave, the weaver will be He. - Rumi

Poem Fifteen

The Full Potential

This poem considers the full potential of awakening using the Bodhisattva path of Mahayana Buddhism as an example. The prerequisite is the recognition of *anatta*, that is that no 'separate self' exists. This consists of ten stages, the name of each is given in hyphens. The first six stages, or *bhumis*, each have a virtue (in italics) that is to be perfected before one moves on to the next one. Parinirvana is the final nirvana after which one is no longer reborn, and maras are demons which one discovers to be purely mind created after one awakens.

The Full Potential

Of awakening what is the full potential?
One cannot say, it's beyond experiential.
To further spiritual deepening there is no end,
Great masters say, on whose words we can depend.

The deeper you go the more you will find,
For what is investigated has no limit defined.
For example, in Mahayana there are ten stages
Of Bhodisattvahood, to be attained over many ages.

The first, 'joyful', where one perfects *giving*,
Governed by compassion to liberate the living.
The second, 'stainless', where *morality* is to be perfected,
Natural to those in whom no 'separate self' is projected.

The third, 'luminous', where *patience* is to be developed,
For those with no-self are never by anger enveloped.
The fourth, 'the radiant', perfecting *vigour* or effort,
Resulting from awakening, where self cannot be sought.

The fifth, 'difficult to overcome' (by the maras), perfecting *meditation*,
Powerless when recognized as mind-forms, without any hesitation.
The sixth, 'face to face', perfecting *wisdom* and gaining total insight.
Spurning parinirvana, aiding humanity to awaken, touched by its plight.

The seventh, 'gone afar', when skilful means are perfected.
The last three, the pure grounds, where no stain is detected.
'Immovable', 'Good Intelligence' and 'The Cloud of Dhamma',
Utterly pristine, transcending knowledge and samsara.

Of awakening this is the Mahayana view,
Giving clues, as this deepens, to what awaits you.
It's encouraging to see that, when staying awake and aware,
The first stage is joyful, after which there is no one to care!

Poem Sixteen

The Best of All Worlds, Humanity at its Peak

Pointing to the fact that if all were to awaken we would be in 'Heaven on Earth'.

The Best of All Worlds, Humanity at its Peak

If with Awareness we identify,

Do we our humanity deny?

Or would our inhumanity

Be replaced by sanity?

When awake we truly become

Full of joy, love and compassion.

We see that no separation exists

For 'All is One', Awareness insists.

Consciousness manifests the universe

And its contents so diverse,

To know Itself, for Its pleasure,

And to reveal 'The Hidden Treasure'.

It needs instruments for sensing and seeing,

The function of every conscious being.

Also to know Itself as consciousness at rest,

Humanity with this potential is blessed.

When awake we can feel the bliss,

Of living, which we generally miss.

Resulting in loving one and all,

On whomsoe'er one's eye may fall.

For Awareness, the lover, consciousness at rest

And the beloved, manifest at its behest,

Are forever one, locked in an eternal embrace

In which no 'parting' can ever take place.

So man's inhumanity to his fellow men

Would totally vanish if all awaken.

Giving 'The Best of All Worlds' that we seek,

Heaven on Earth, Humanity at its peak!

Poems Seventeen and Eighteen

'This' and 'That'

'This' and 'That' are both epithets for Universal Consciousness, - Awareness when at rest and Cosmic Energy when in motion.

This

I am This.
You are This.
We are This.

All is This.
Just This is.
Only This.

Thus,
No fuss,
Or us.

Not two,
Nor you,
Or Who?

Just One,
It's Done.
Must run …

Have Fun!

That

I am That.
You are That.
We are That.

All is That.
Only That.
Om Tat Sat.*

So no,
Need to know,
Or where to go.

As well,
No Heaven
Or Hell.

That's the Tao;
No why or how?
Or Sacred Cow!

Just Be Here Now

…

* Sanskrit: 'That is the only Reality'

www.ingramcontent.com/pod-product-compliance
Lightning Source LLC
Chambersburg PA
CBHW031426040426
42444CB00006B/701